TEACHER:

SCHOOL:

GRADE & ROOM:

PHONE & EMAIL:

CONTENTS

PETER PAUPER PRESS, INC.
White Plains, New York

For Week ______________________________ to ______________________________

SUBJECT	MONDAY	TUESDAY	WEDNESDAY

THURSDAY	FRIDAY	NOTES

For Week ______________________ to ______________________

SUBJECT	MONDAY	TUESDAY	WEDNESDAY

THURSDAY	FRIDAY	NOTES

For Week ______________________ to ______________________

SUBJECT	MONDAY	TUESDAY	WEDNESDAY

THURSDAY	FRIDAY	NOTES

For Week ______________________ to ______________________

SUBJECT	MONDAY	TUESDAY	WEDNESDAY

THURSDAY	FRIDAY	NOTES

For Week ______________________ to ______________________

SUBJECT	MONDAY	TUESDAY	WEDNESDAY

THURSDAY	FRIDAY	NOTES

For Week ______________________________ to ______________________________

SUBJECT	MONDAY	TUESDAY	WEDNESDAY

THURSDAY	FRIDAY	NOTES

For Week ______________________ to ______________________

SUBJECT	MONDAY	TUESDAY	WEDNESDAY

THURSDAY	FRIDAY	NOTES

For Week ________________________ to ________________________

SUBJECT	MONDAY	TUESDAY	WEDNESDAY

THURSDAY	FRIDAY	NOTES

For Week ______________________ to ______________________

SUBJECT	MONDAY	TUESDAY	WEDNESDAY

THURSDAY	FRIDAY	NOTES

For Week ______________________ to ______________________

SUBJECT	MONDAY	TUESDAY	WEDNESDAY

THURSDAY	FRIDAY	NOTES

For Week ______________________ to ______________________

SUBJECT	MONDAY	TUESDAY	WEDNESDAY

THURSDAY	FRIDAY	NOTES

For Week ____________________ to ____________________

SUBJECT	MONDAY	TUESDAY	WEDNESDAY

THURSDAY	FRIDAY	NOTES

For Week ______________________________ to ______________________________

SUBJECT	MONDAY	TUESDAY	WEDNESDAY

THURSDAY	FRIDAY	NOTES

For Week ____________________ to ____________________

SUBJECT	MONDAY	TUESDAY	WEDNESDAY

THURSDAY	FRIDAY	NOTES

For Week ______________________ to ______________________

SUBJECT	MONDAY	TUESDAY	WEDNESDAY

THURSDAY	FRIDAY	NOTES

For Week ______________________ to ______________________

SUBJECT	MONDAY	TUESDAY	WEDNESDAY

THURSDAY	FRIDAY	NOTES

For Week ________________________ to ________________________

SUBJECT	MONDAY	TUESDAY	WEDNESDAY

THURSDAY	FRIDAY	NOTES

For Week ______________________ to ______________________

SUBJECT	MONDAY	TUESDAY	WEDNESDAY

THURSDAY	FRIDAY	NOTES

For Week ____________________ to ____________________

SUBJECT	MONDAY	TUESDAY	WEDNESDAY

THURSDAY	FRIDAY	NOTES

For Week ______________________ to ______________________

SUBJECT	MONDAY	TUESDAY	WEDNESDAY

THURSDAY	FRIDAY	NOTES

For Week ______________________ to ______________________

SUBJECT	MONDAY	TUESDAY	WEDNESDAY

THURSDAY	FRIDAY	NOTES

For Week ______________________ to ______________________

SUBJECT	MONDAY	TUESDAY	WEDNESDAY

THURSDAY	FRIDAY	NOTES

For Week ______________________ to ______________________

SUBJECT	MONDAY	TUESDAY	WEDNESDAY

THURSDAY	FRIDAY	NOTES

For Week ____________________ to ____________________

SUBJECT	MONDAY	TUESDAY	WEDNESDAY

THURSDAY	FRIDAY	NOTES

For Week ______________________ to ______________________

SUBJECT	MONDAY	TUESDAY	WEDNESDAY

THURSDAY	FRIDAY	NOTES

For Week ______________________ to ______________________

SUBJECT	MONDAY	TUESDAY	WEDNESDAY

THURSDAY	FRIDAY	NOTES

For Week ______________________ to ______________________

SUBJECT	MONDAY	TUESDAY	WEDNESDAY

THURSDAY	FRIDAY	NOTES

For Week ______________________ to ______________________

SUBJECT	MONDAY	TUESDAY	WEDNESDAY

THURSDAY	FRIDAY	NOTES

For Week ______________________ to ______________________

SUBJECT	MONDAY	TUESDAY	WEDNESDAY

THURSDAY	FRIDAY	NOTES

For Week ________________________ to ________________________

SUBJECT	MONDAY	TUESDAY	WEDNESDAY

THURSDAY	FRIDAY	NOTES

For Week ________________________ to ________________________

SUBJECT	MONDAY	TUESDAY	WEDNESDAY

THURSDAY	FRIDAY	NOTES

For Week ______________________________ to ______________________________

SUBJECT	MONDAY	TUESDAY	WEDNESDAY

THURSDAY	FRIDAY	NOTES

For Week ______________________ to ______________________

SUBJECT	MONDAY	TUESDAY	WEDNESDAY

THURSDAY	FRIDAY	NOTES

For Week ______________________________ to ______________________________

SUBJECT	MONDAY	TUESDAY	WEDNESDAY

THURSDAY	FRIDAY	NOTES

For Week ______________________________ to ______________________________

SUBJECT	MONDAY	TUESDAY	WEDNESDAY

THURSDAY	FRIDAY	NOTES

For Week ______________________ to ______________________

SUBJECT	MONDAY	TUESDAY	WEDNESDAY

THURSDAY	FRIDAY	NOTES

For Week ______________________________ to ______________________________

SUBJECT	MONDAY	TUESDAY	WEDNESDAY

THURSDAY	FRIDAY	NOTES

For Week ______________________ to ______________________

SUBJECT	MONDAY	TUESDAY	WEDNESDAY

THURSDAY	FRIDAY	NOTES

For Week ______________________________ to ______________________________

SUBJECT	MONDAY	TUESDAY	WEDNESDAY

THURSDAY	FRIDAY	NOTES

For Week ____________________ to ____________________

SUBJECT	MONDAY	TUESDAY	WEDNESDAY

THURSDAY	FRIDAY	NOTES

For Week ______________________________ to ______________________________

SUBJECT	MONDAY	TUESDAY	WEDNESDAY

THURSDAY	FRIDAY	NOTES

For Week ______________________ to ______________________

SUBJECT	MONDAY	TUESDAY	WEDNESDAY

THURSDAY	FRIDAY	NOTES

For Week ______________________ to ______________________

SUBJECT	MONDAY	TUESDAY	WEDNESDAY

THURSDAY	FRIDAY	NOTES

For Week ______________________ to ______________________

SUBJECT	MONDAY	TUESDAY	WEDNESDAY

THURSDAY	FRIDAY	NOTES

For Week ______________________________ to ______________________________

SUBJECT	MONDAY	TUESDAY	WEDNESDAY

THURSDAY	FRIDAY	NOTES

SEATING CHART

SEATING CHART

SEATING CHART

SEATING CHART

ATTENDANCE OR GRADES

NAME

ATTENDANCE OR GRADES

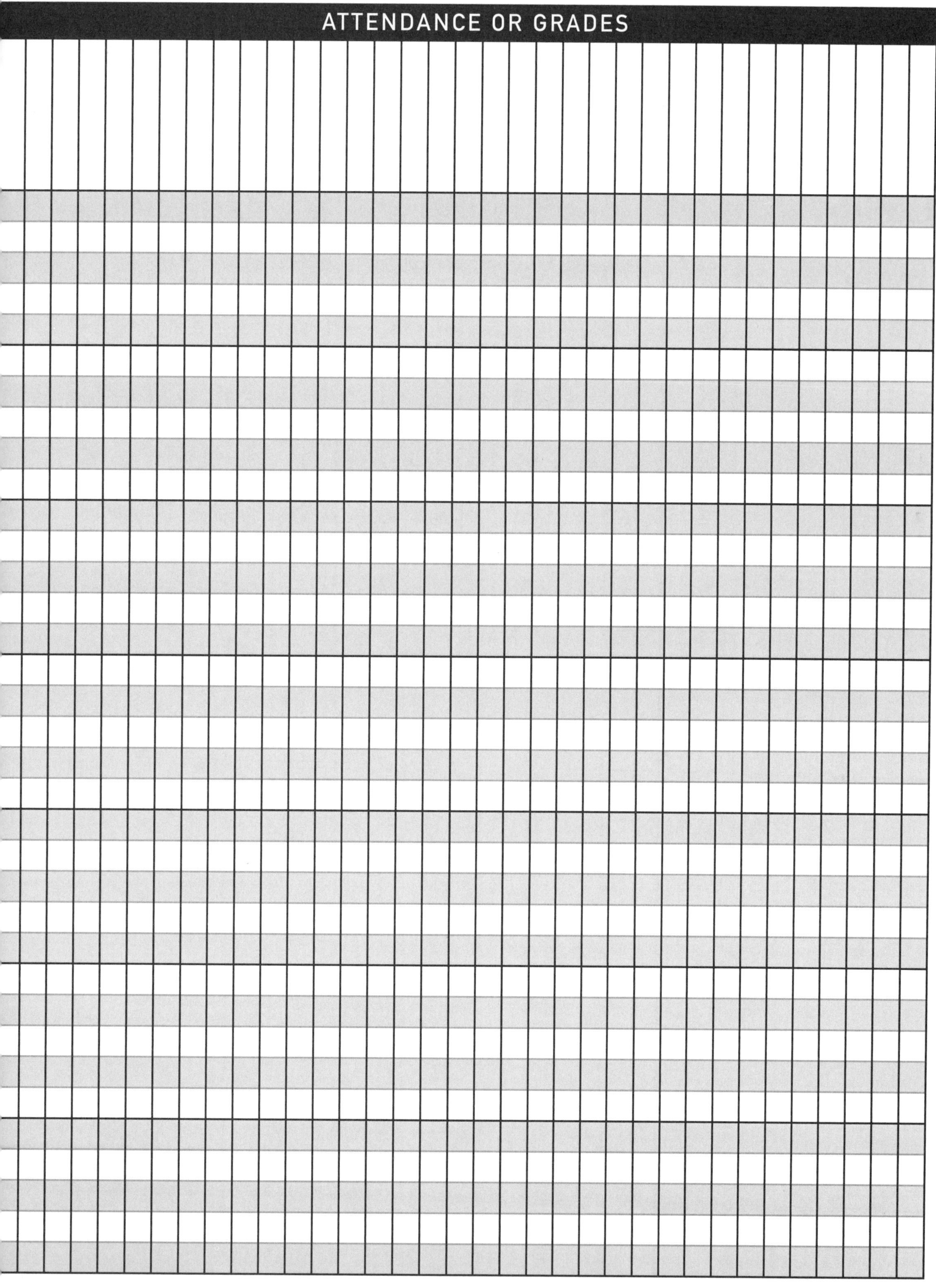

ATTENDANCE OR GRADES

NAME

ATTENDANCE OR GRADES

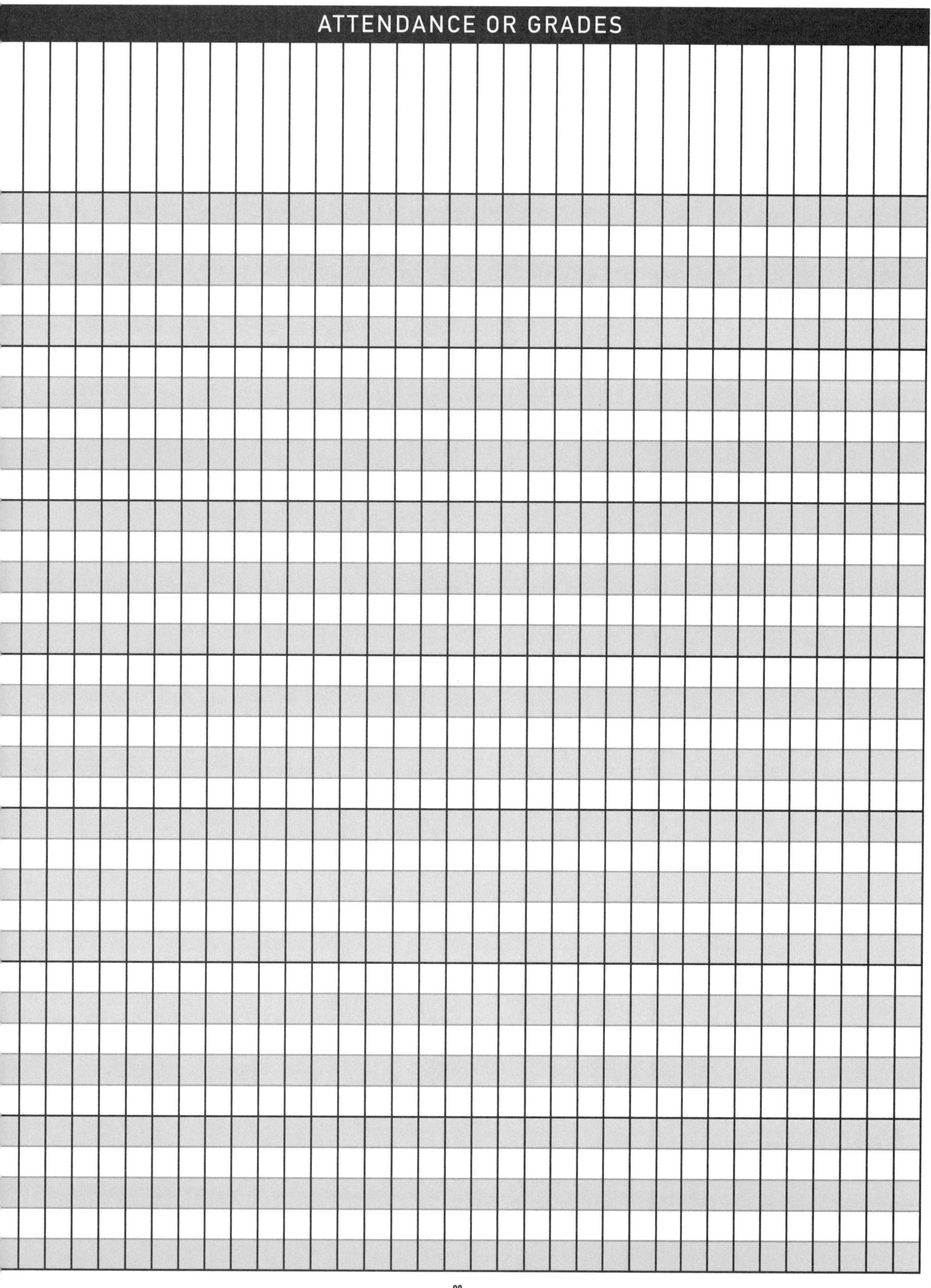

NAME	ATTENDANCE OR GRADES

ATTENDANCE OR GRADES

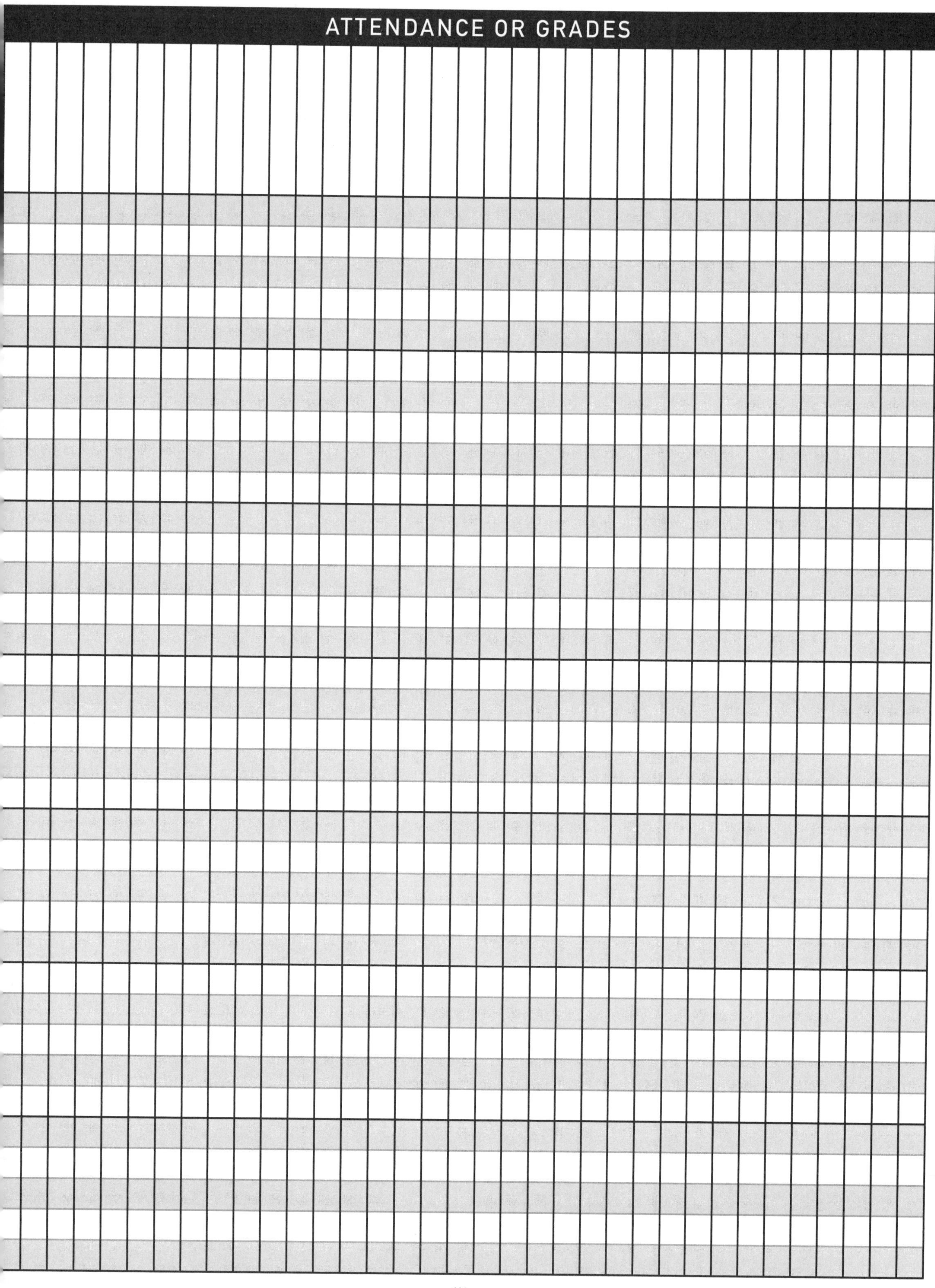

NAME	ATTENDANCE OR GRADES

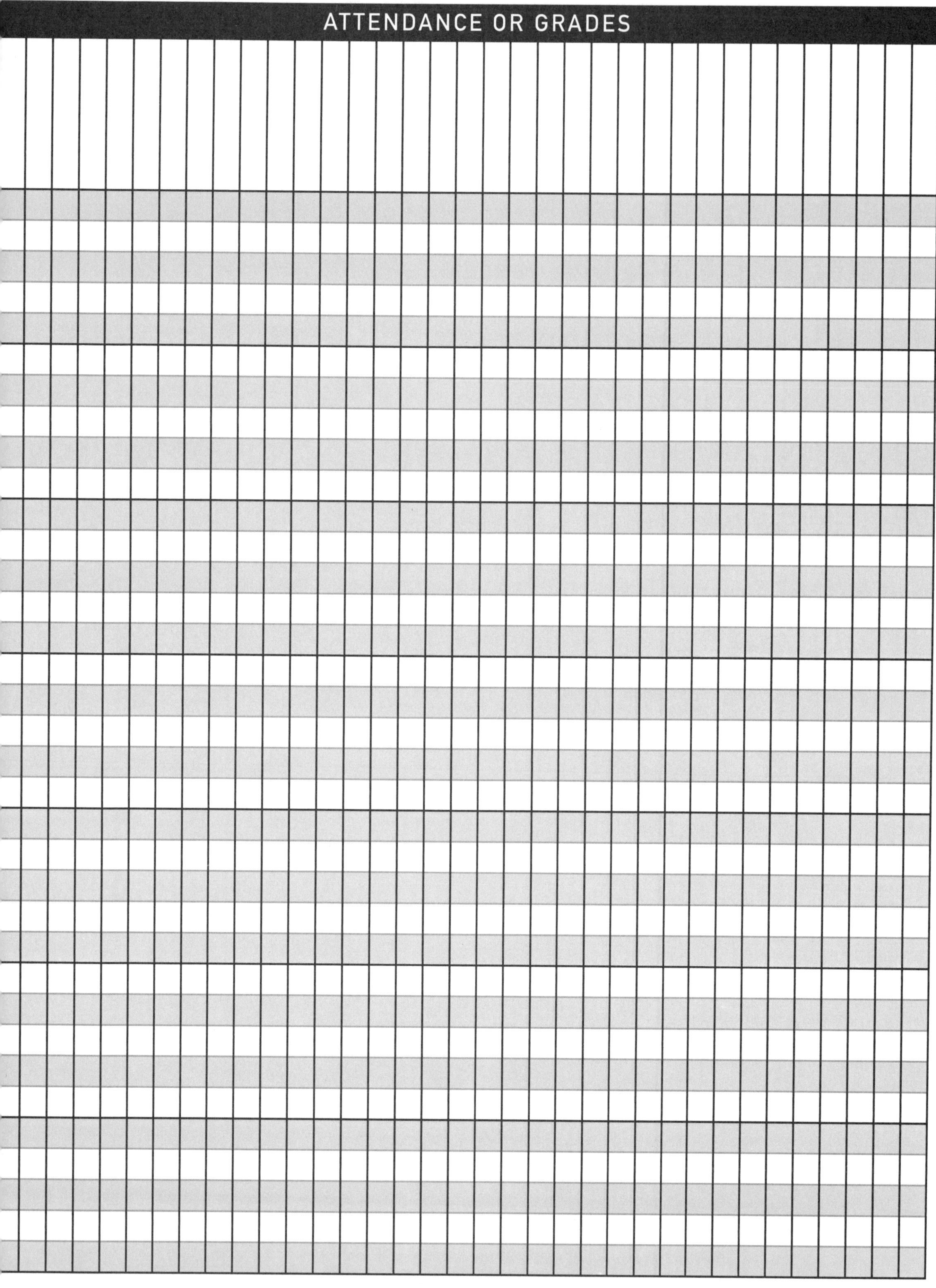
ATTENDANCE OR GRADES

ATTENDANCE OR GRADES

NAME

ATTENDANCE OR GRADES

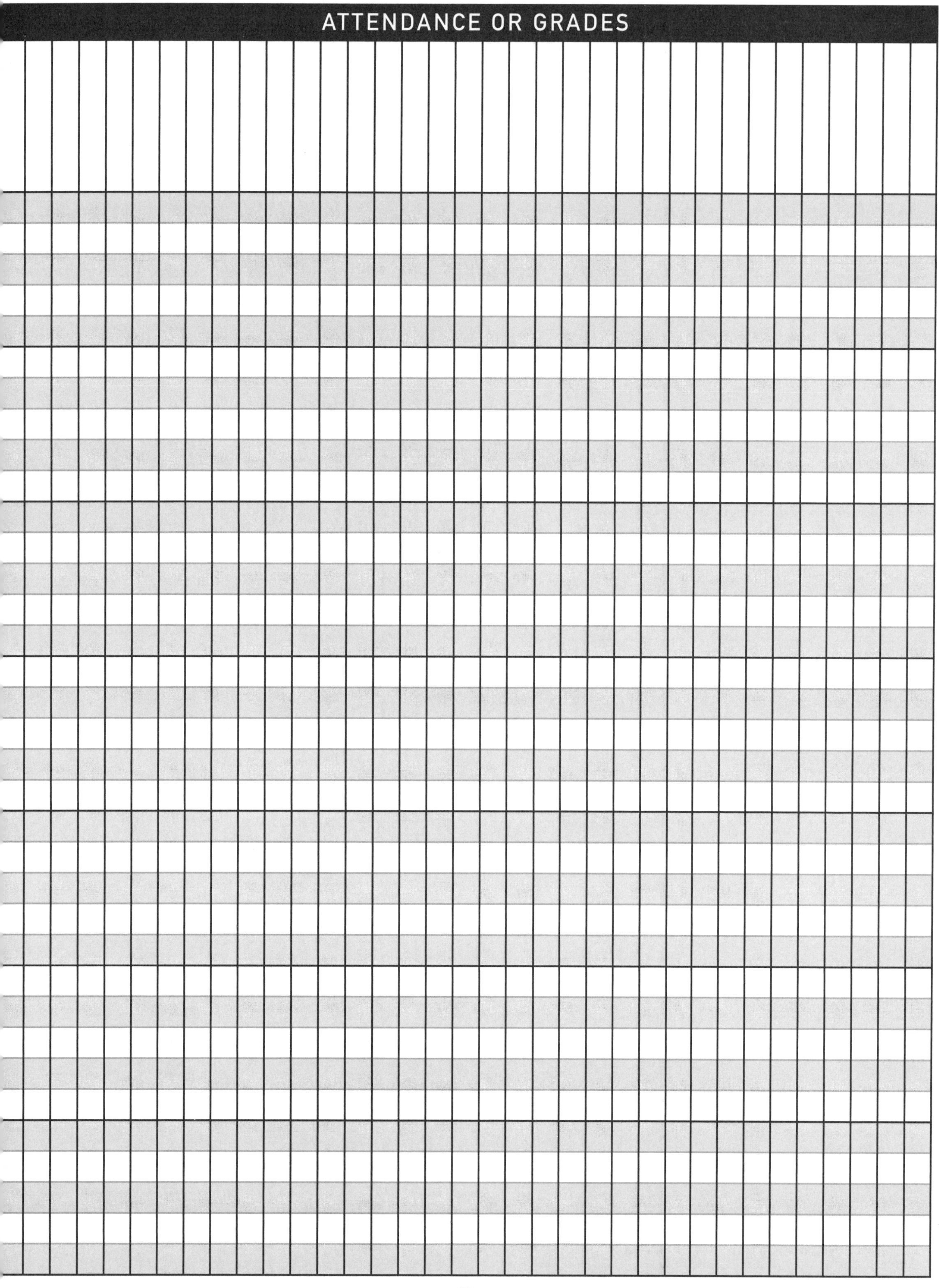

ATTENDANCE OR GRADES

NAME

ATTENDANCE OR GRADES

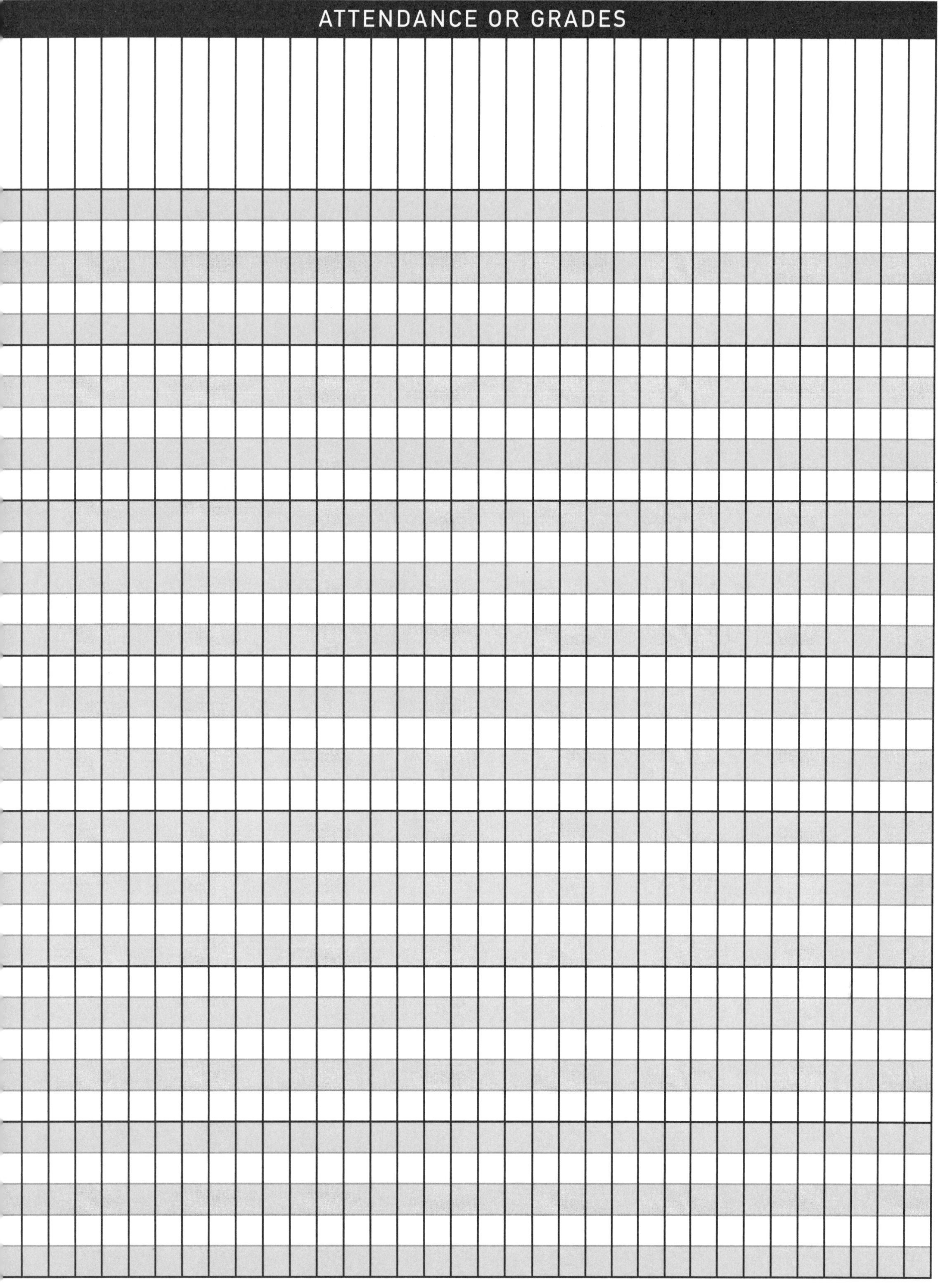

ATTENDANCE OR GRADES

NAME

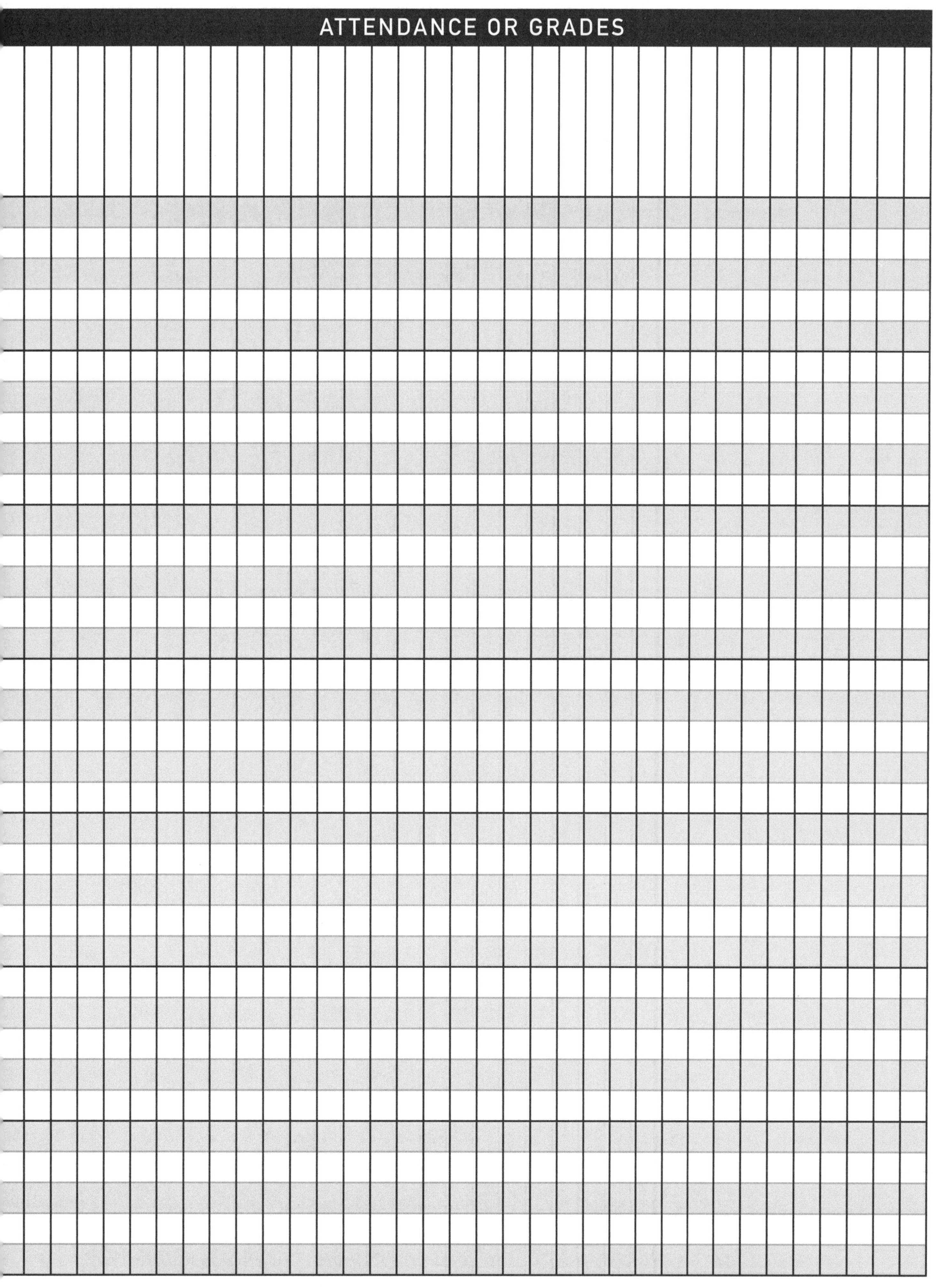

ATTENDANCE OR GRADES

NAME

ATTENDANCE OR GRADES

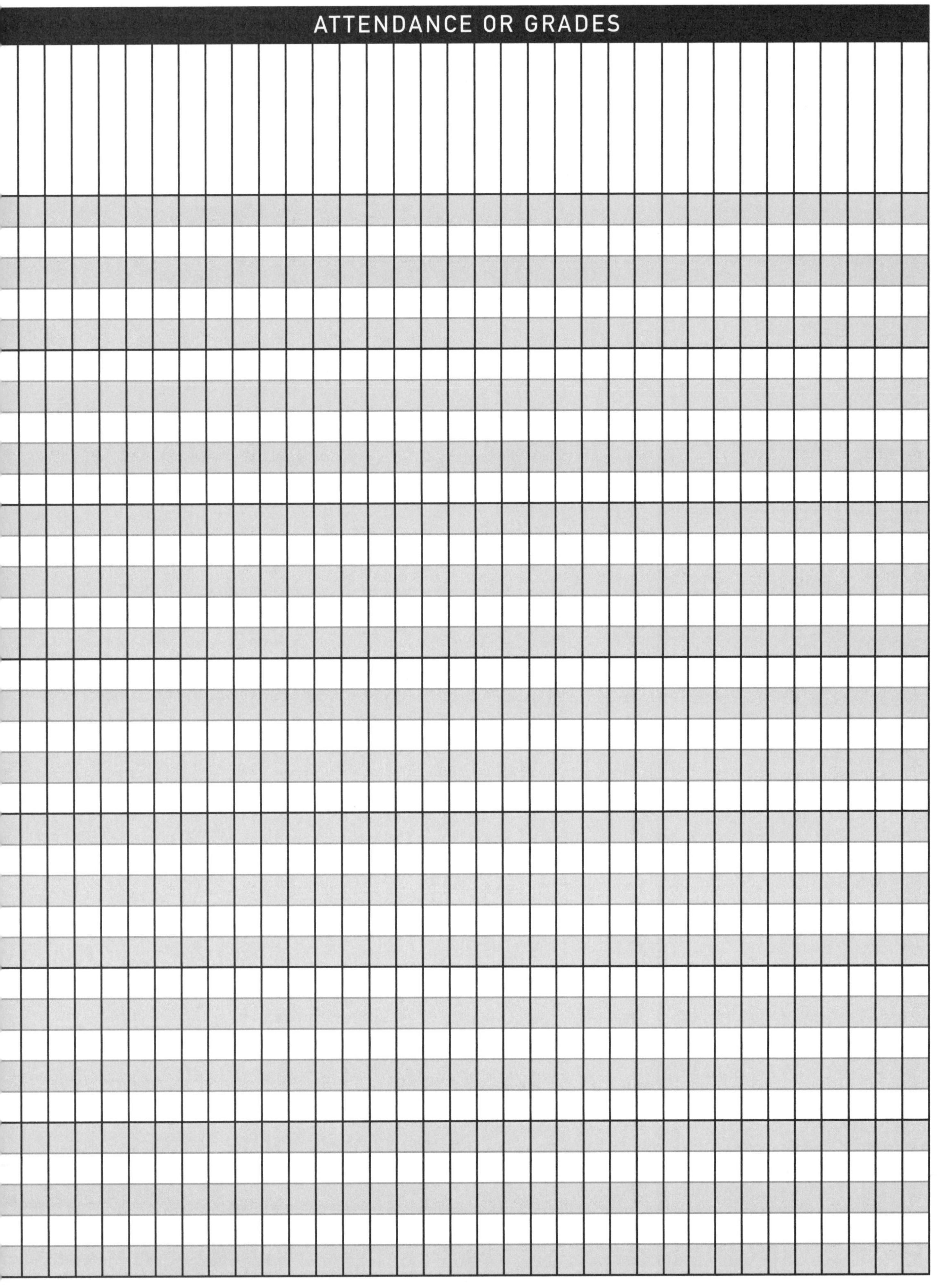

ATTENDANCE OR GRADES

NAME

ATTENDANCE OR GRADES

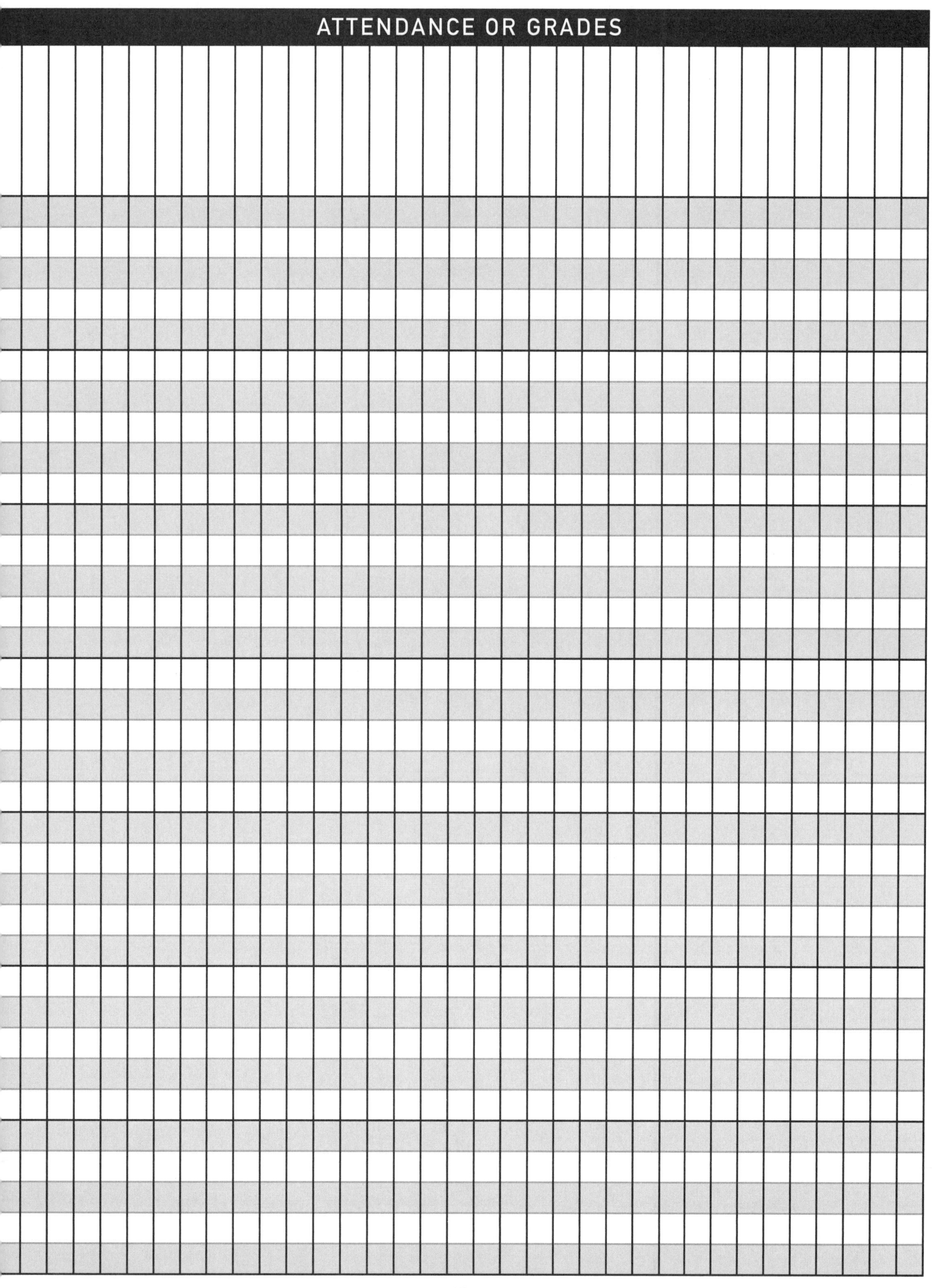

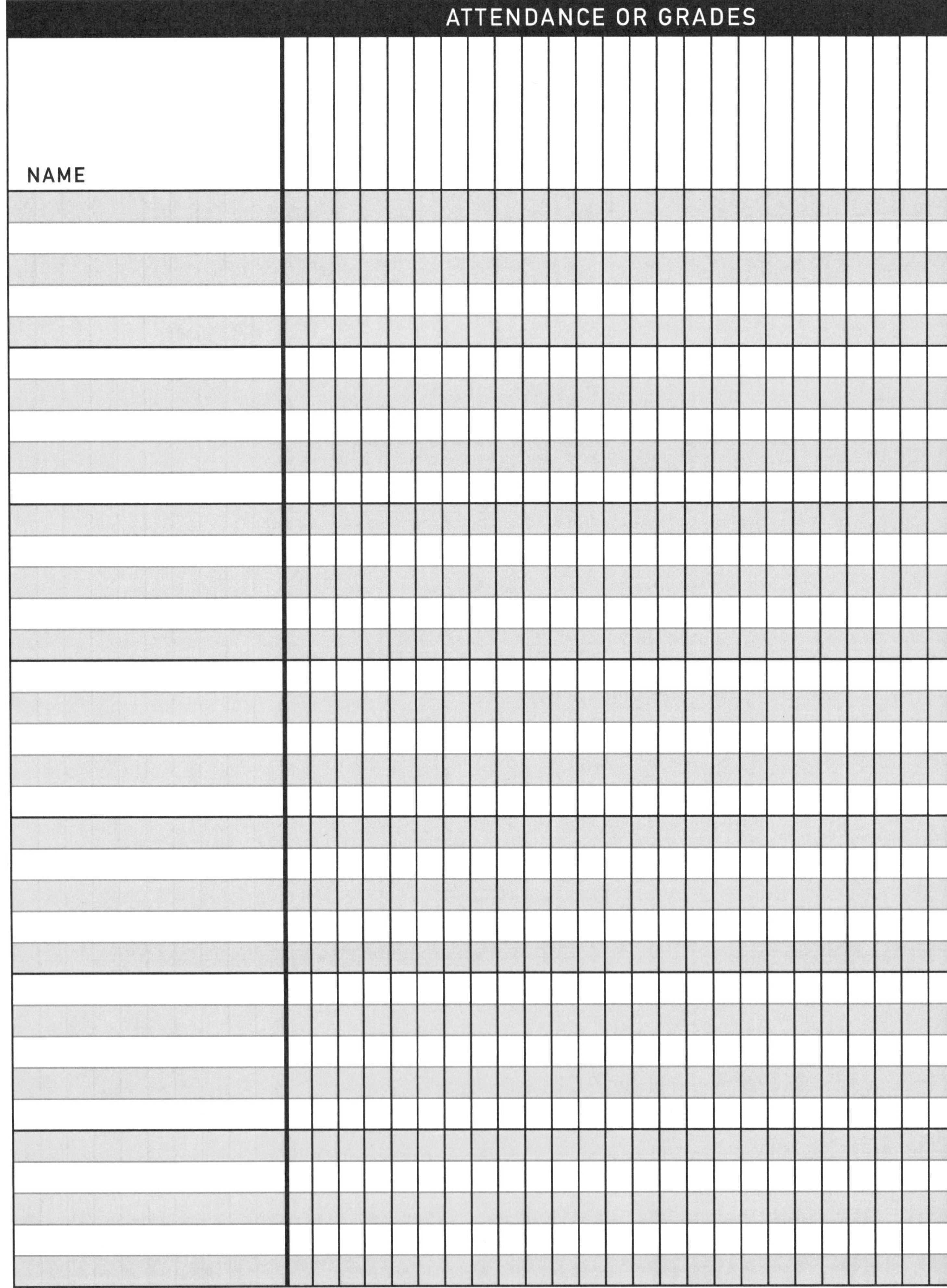
ATTENDANCE OR GRADES
NAME

ATTENDANCE OR GRADES

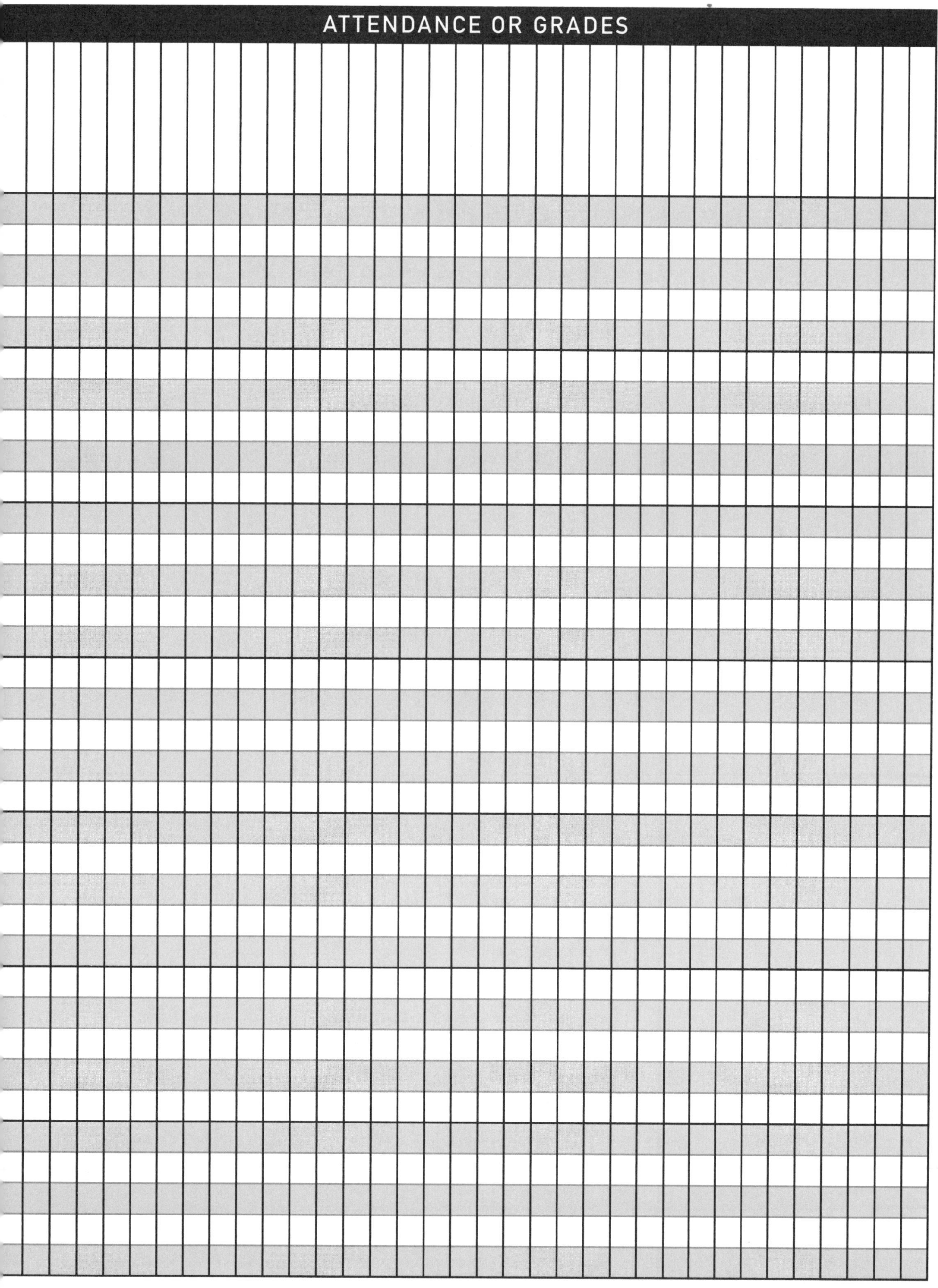

ATTENDANCE OR GRADES

NAME

ATTENDANCE OR GRADES

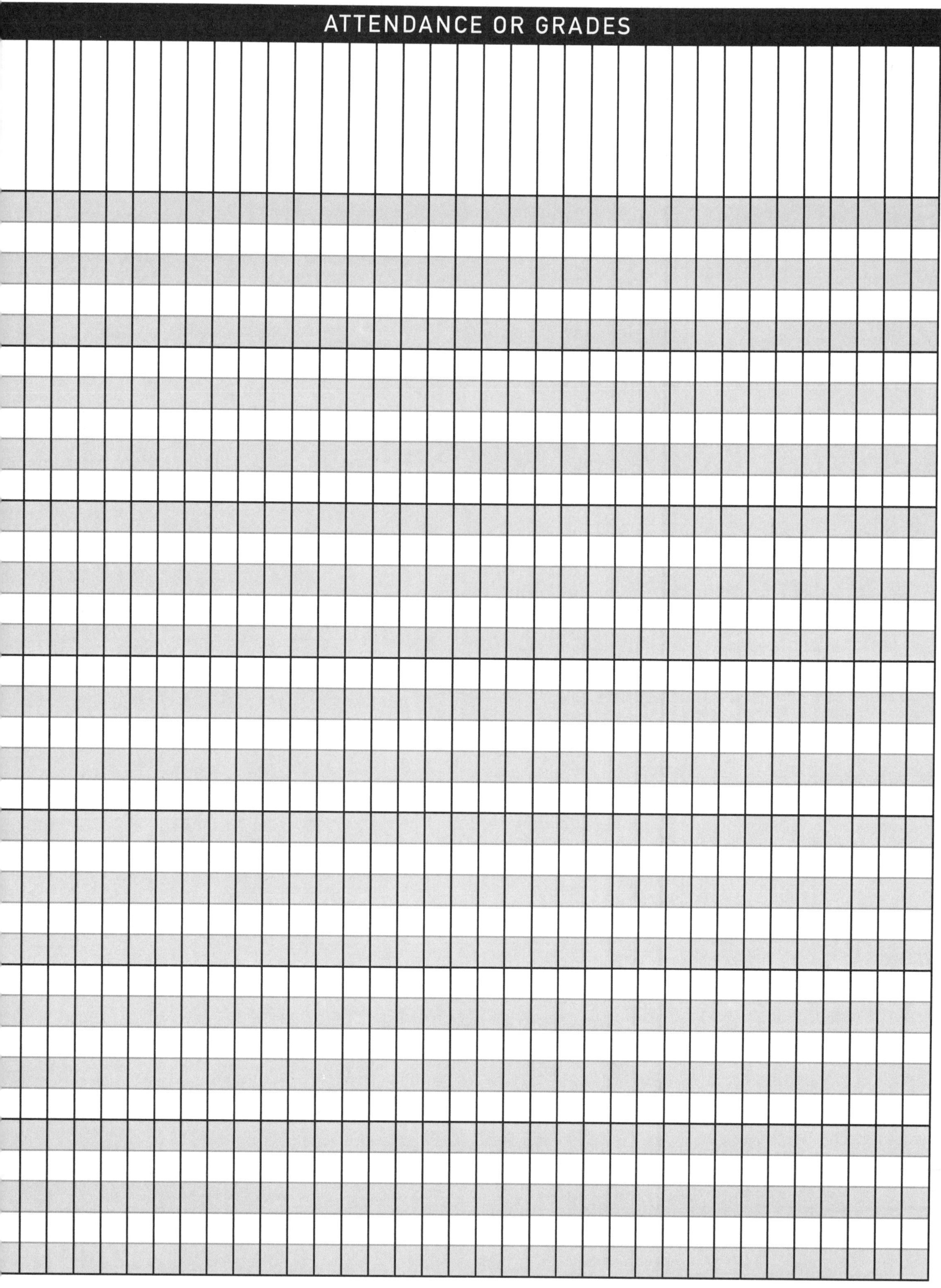

ATTENDANCE OR GRADES

NAME

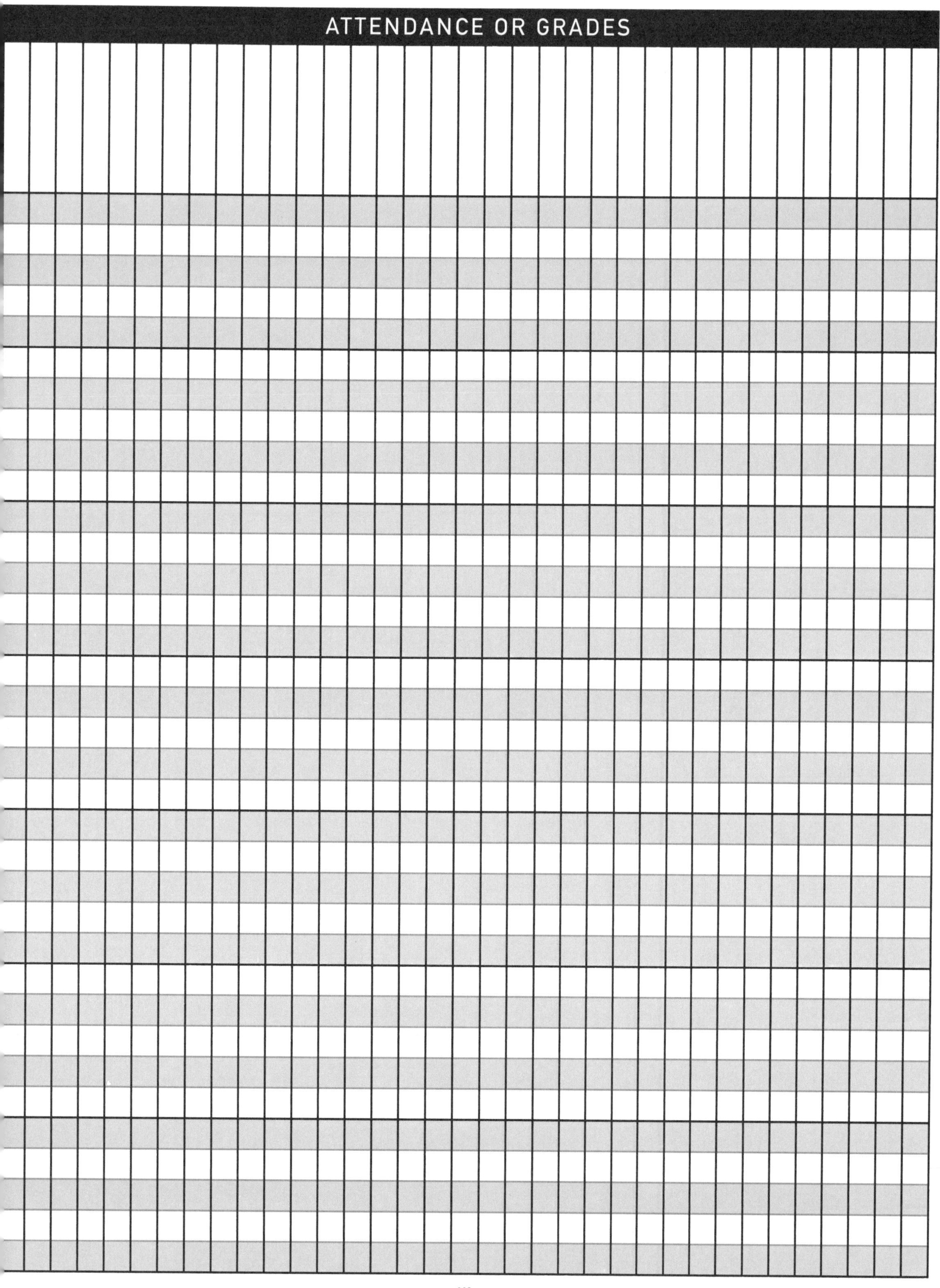
ATTENDANCE OR GRADES

NAME	ATTENDANCE OR GRADES

ATTENDANCE OR GRADES

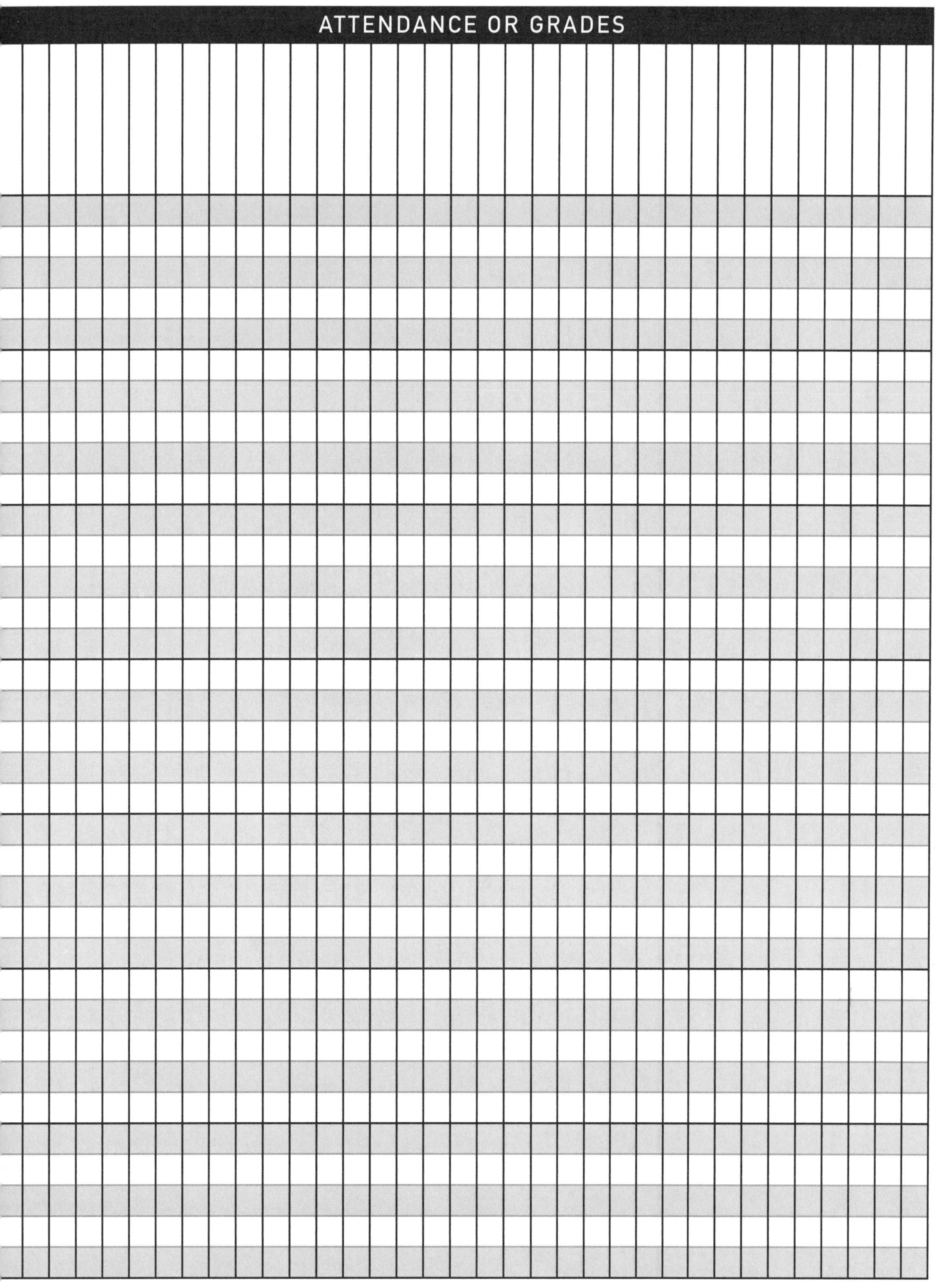

ATTENDANCE OR GRADES

NAME

ATTENDANCE OR GRADES

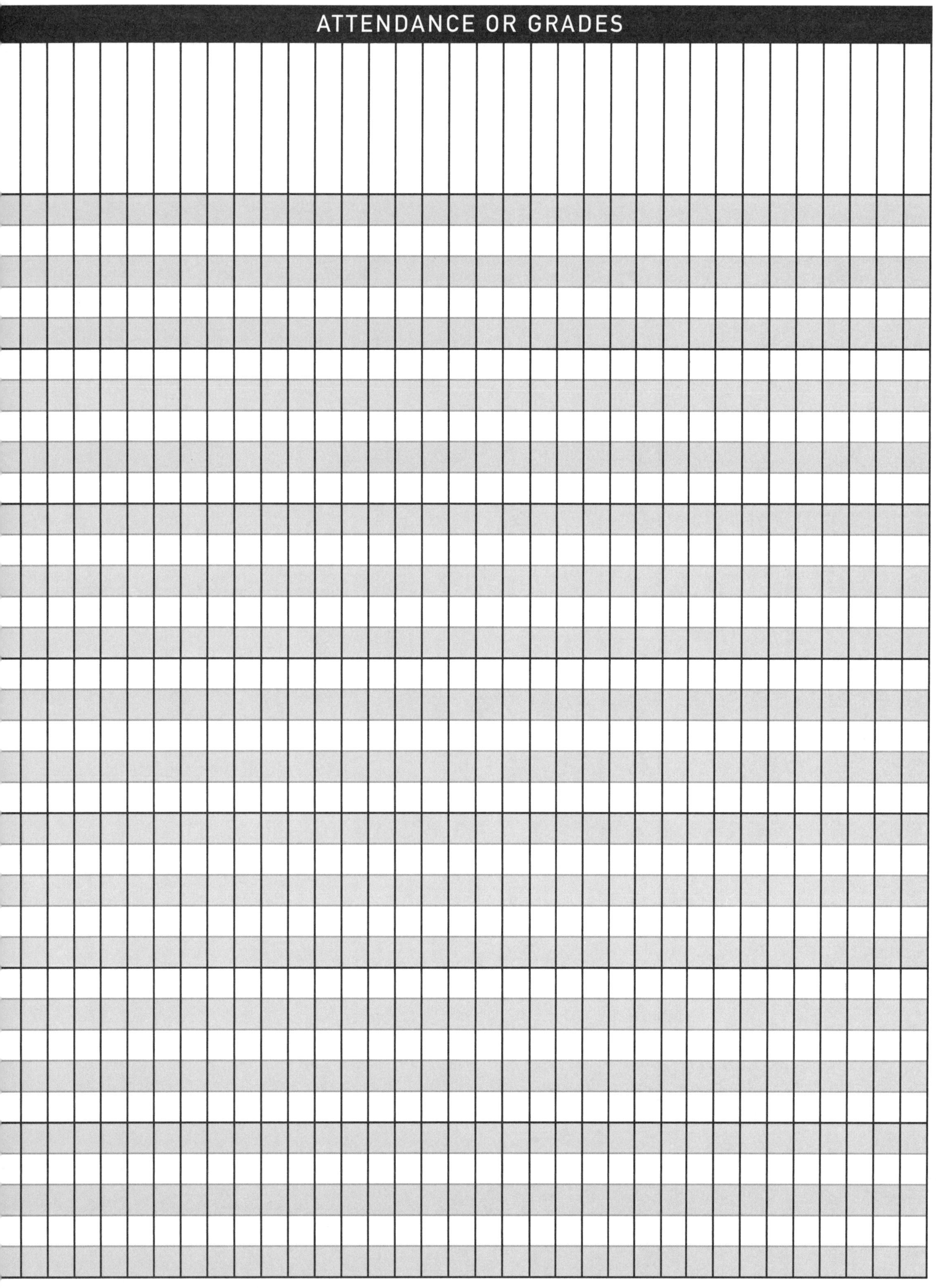

ATTENDANCE OR GRADES

NAME

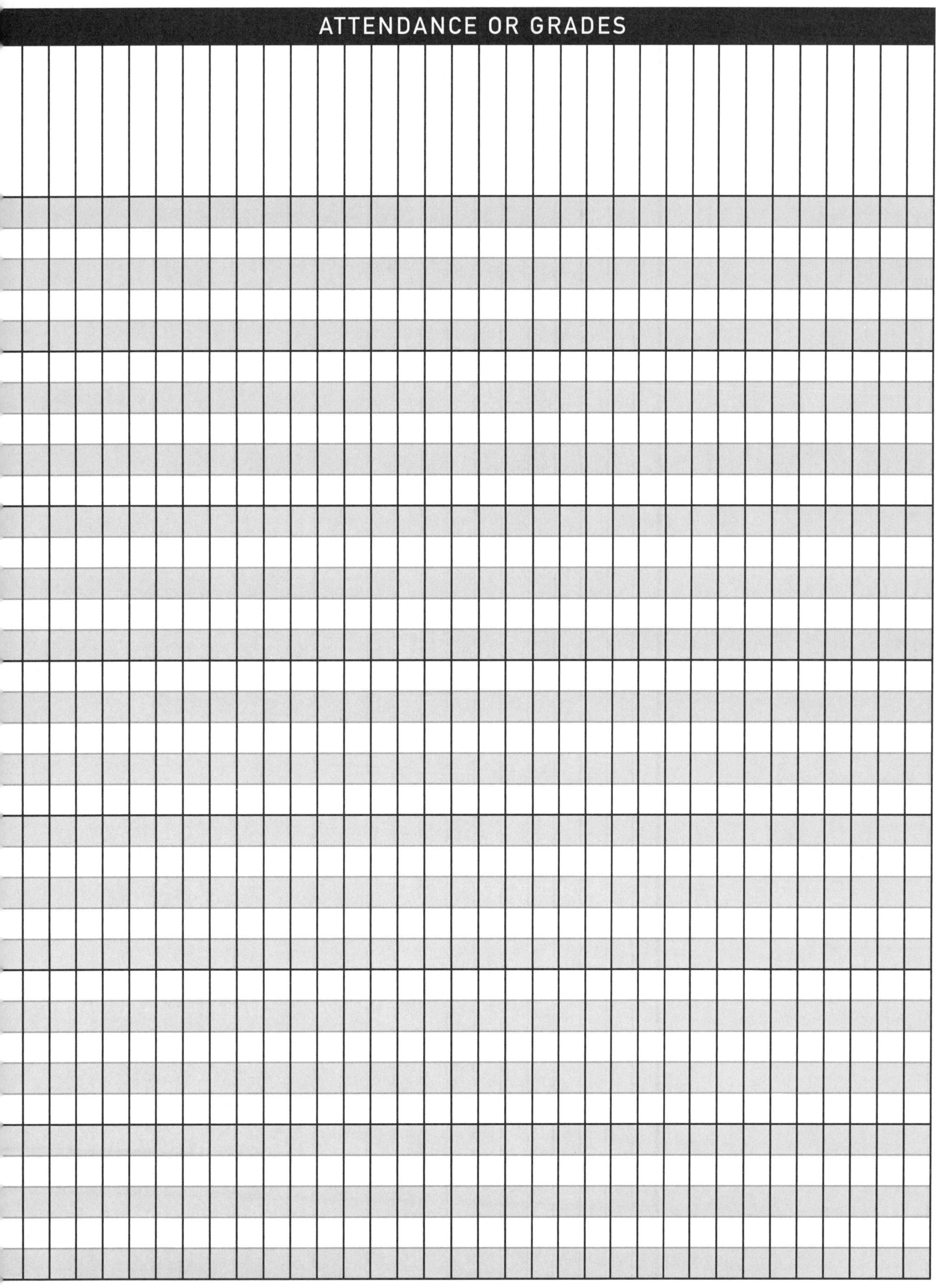

ATTENDANCE OR GRADES

NAME

ATTENDANCE OR GRADES

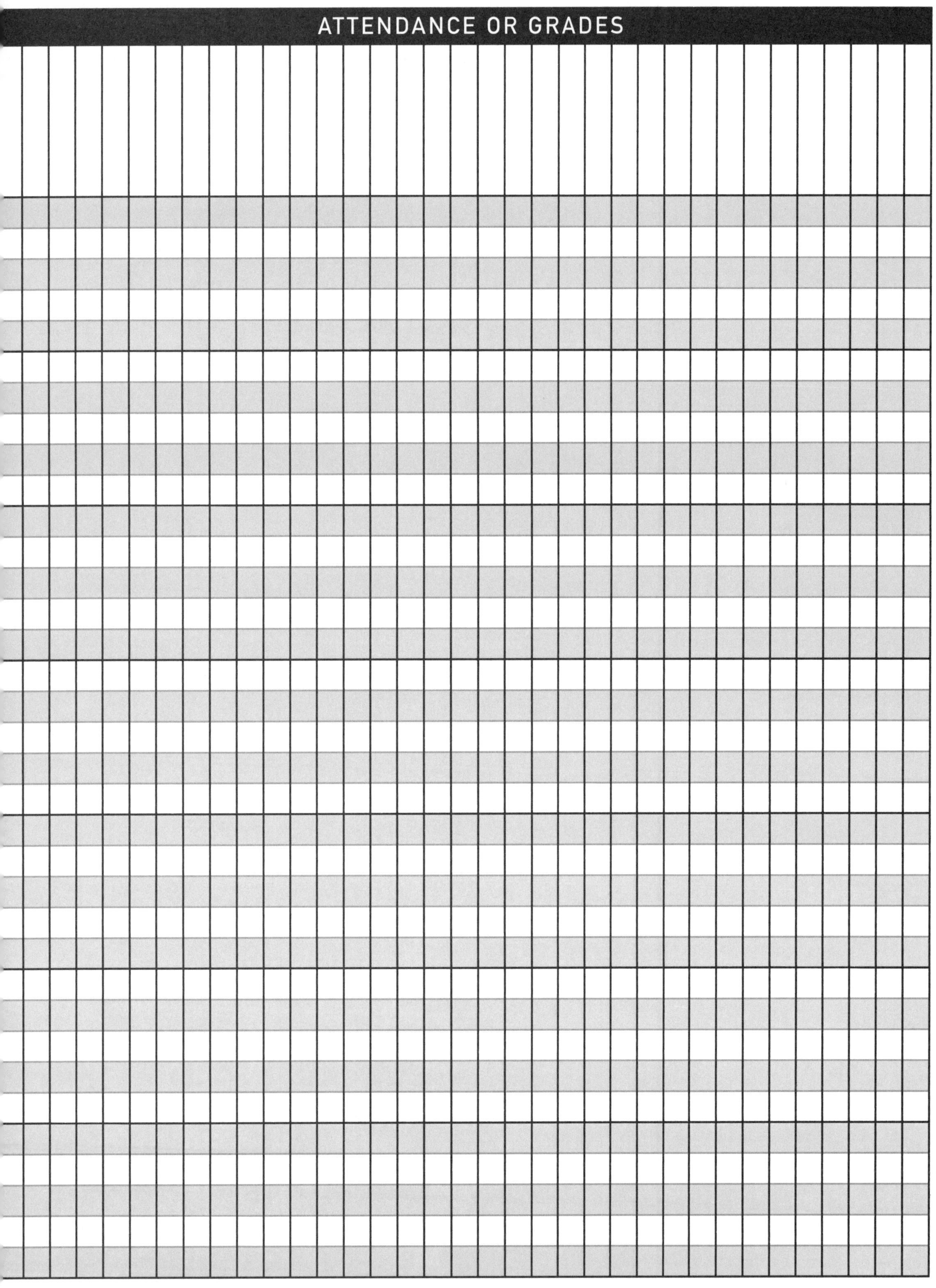

ATTENDANCE OR GRADES

NAME

ATTENDANCE OR GRADES

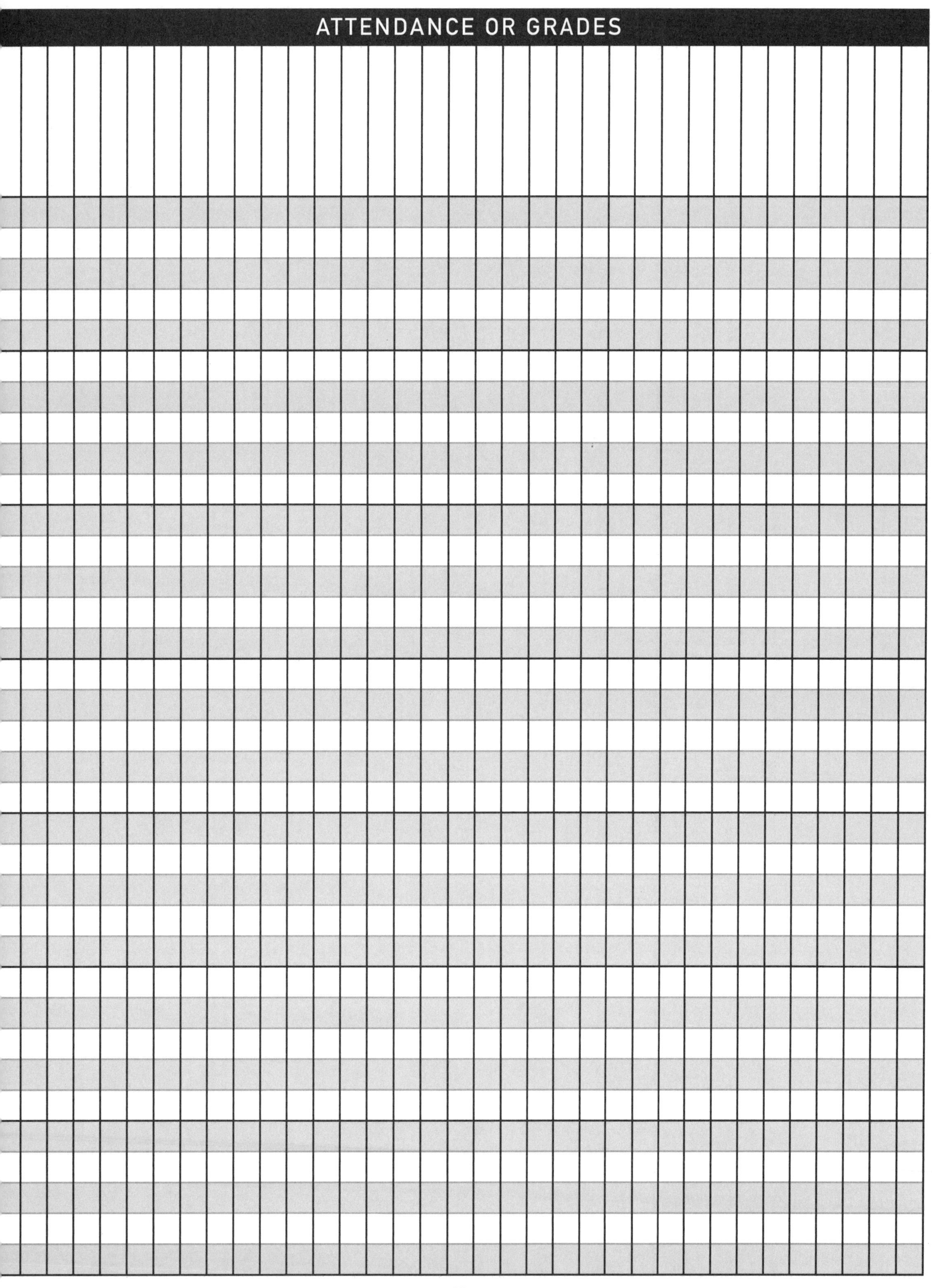

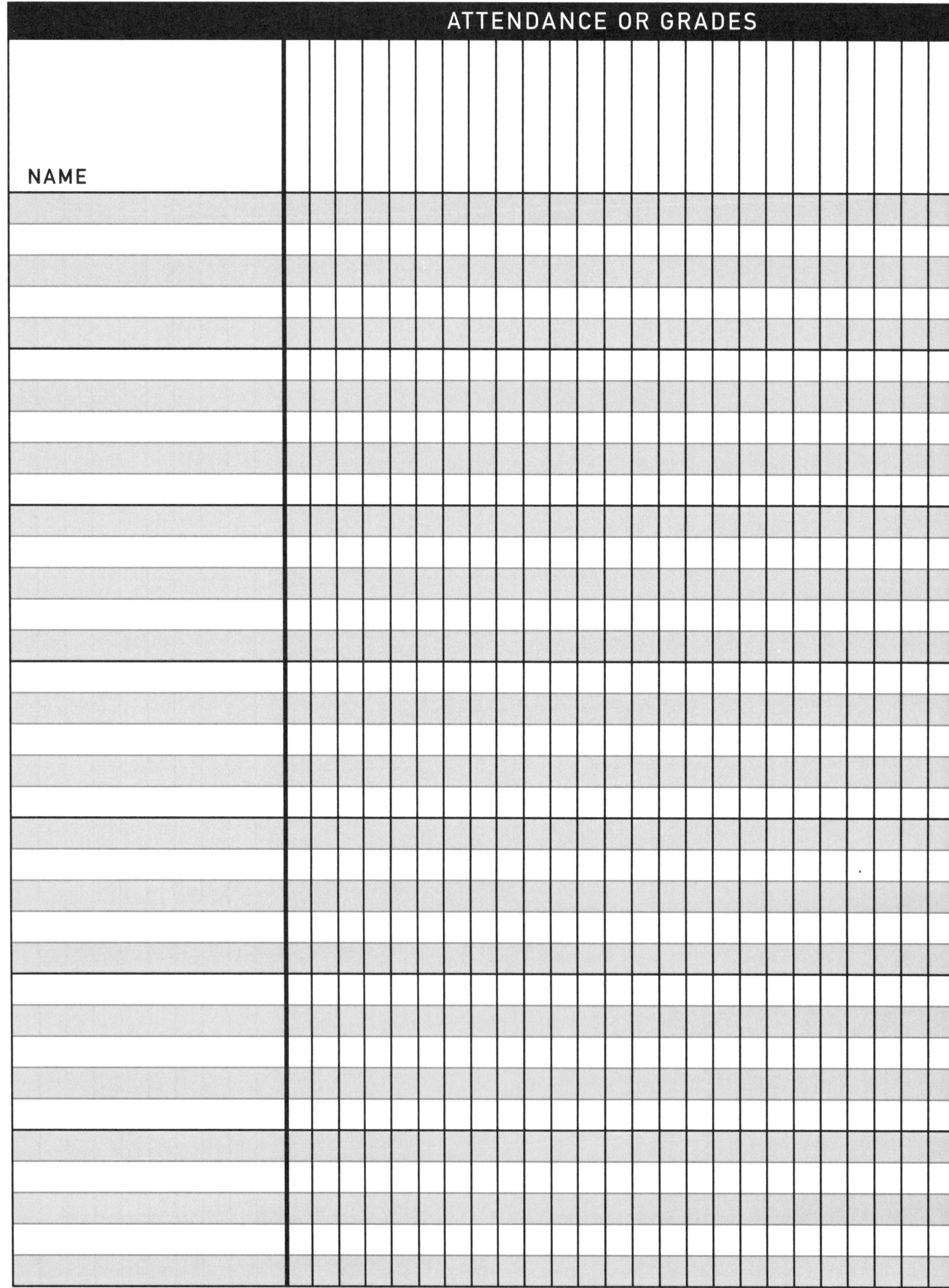

ATTENDANCE OR GRADES

NAME

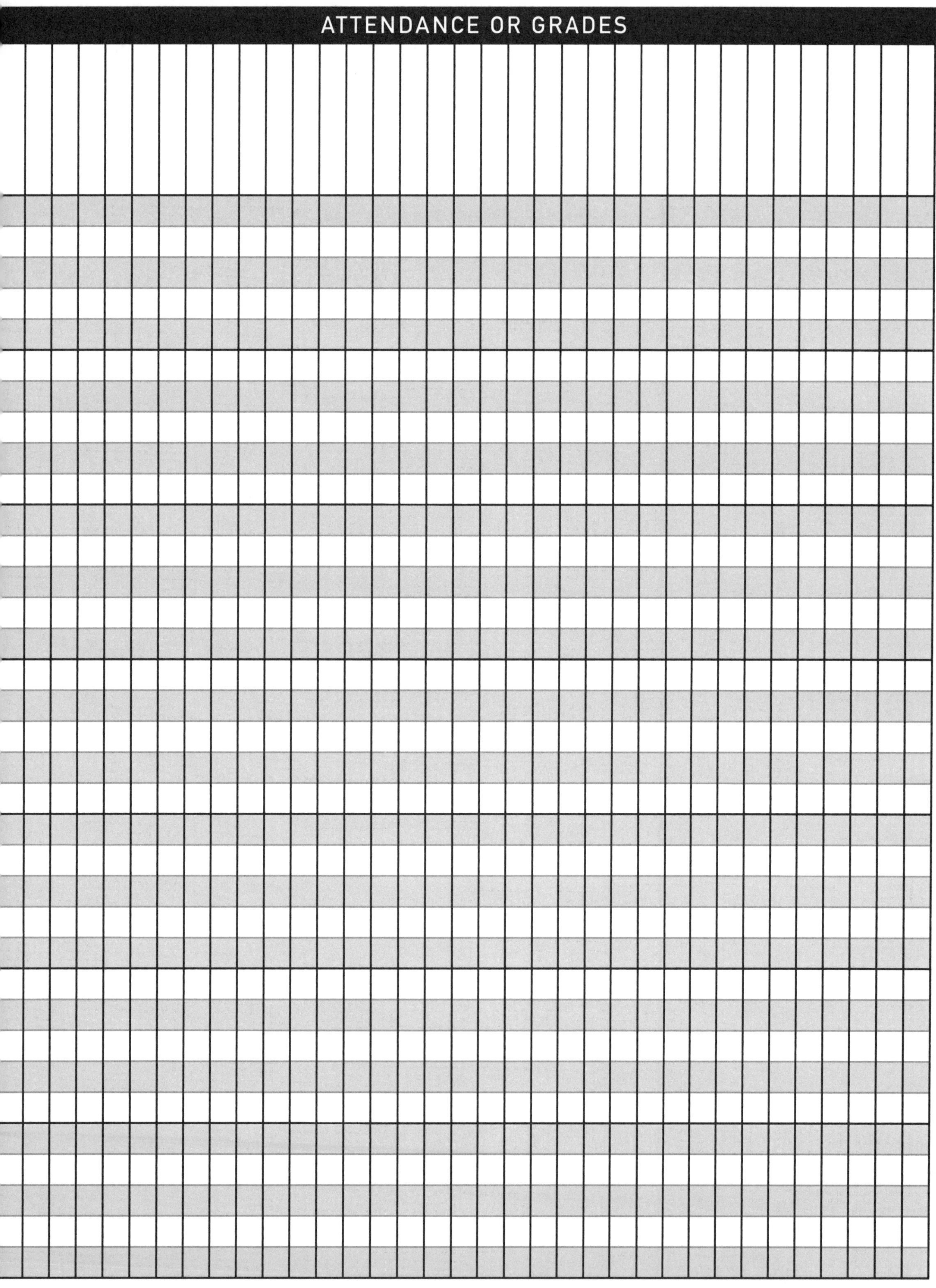

NAME	ATTENDANCE OR GRADES

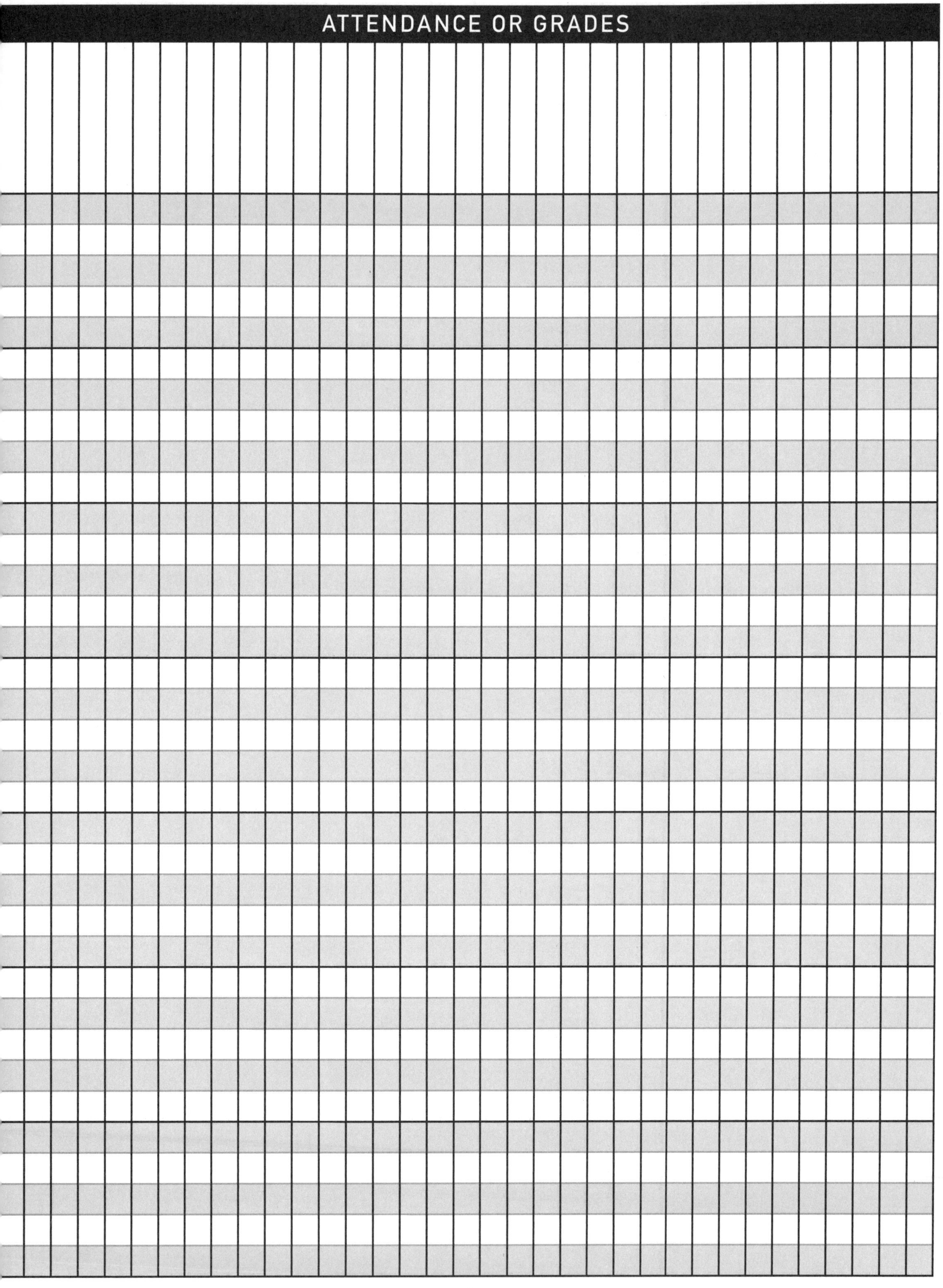

ATTENDANCE OR GRADES

NAME

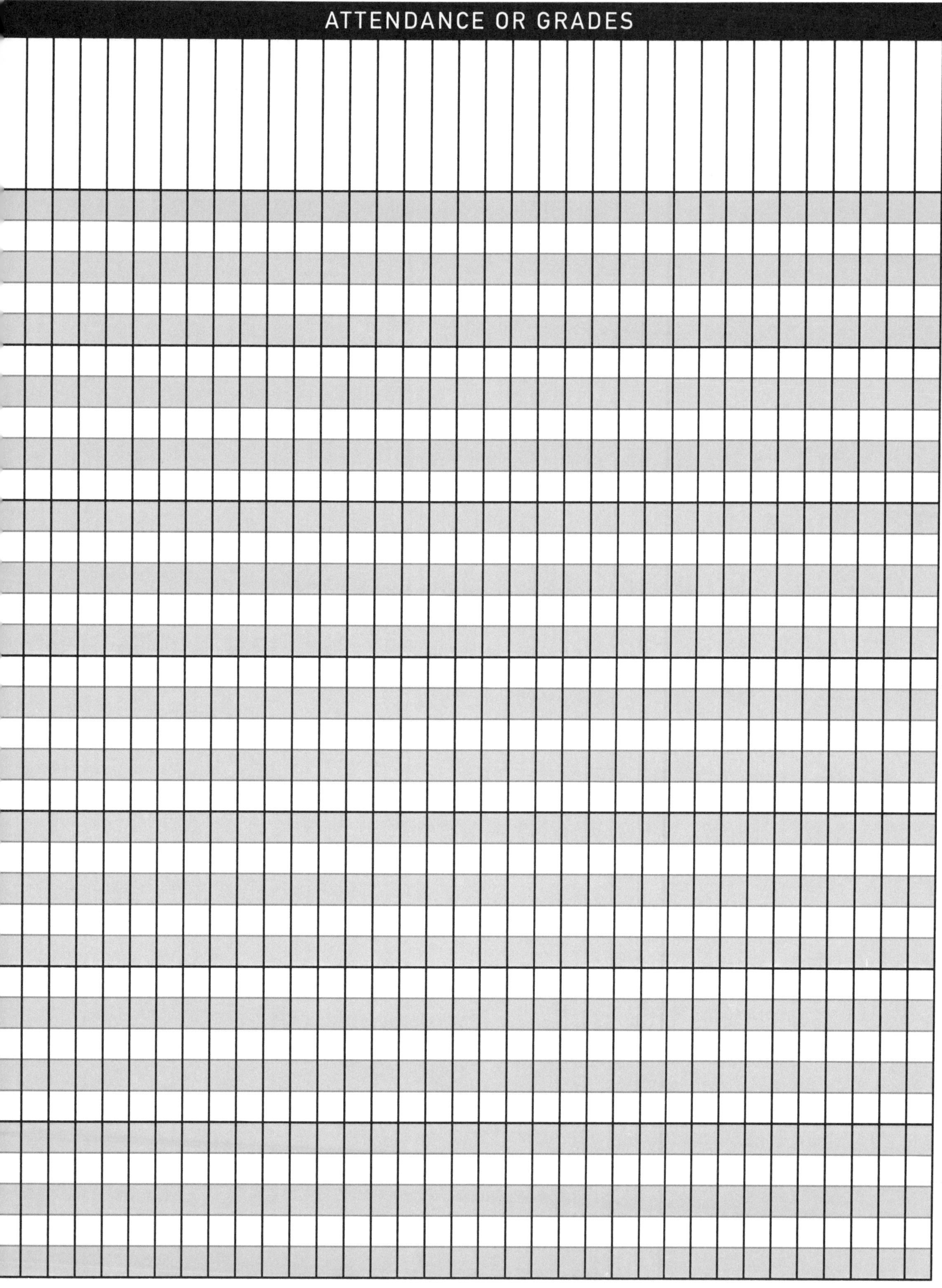

ATTENDANCE OR GRADES

NAME

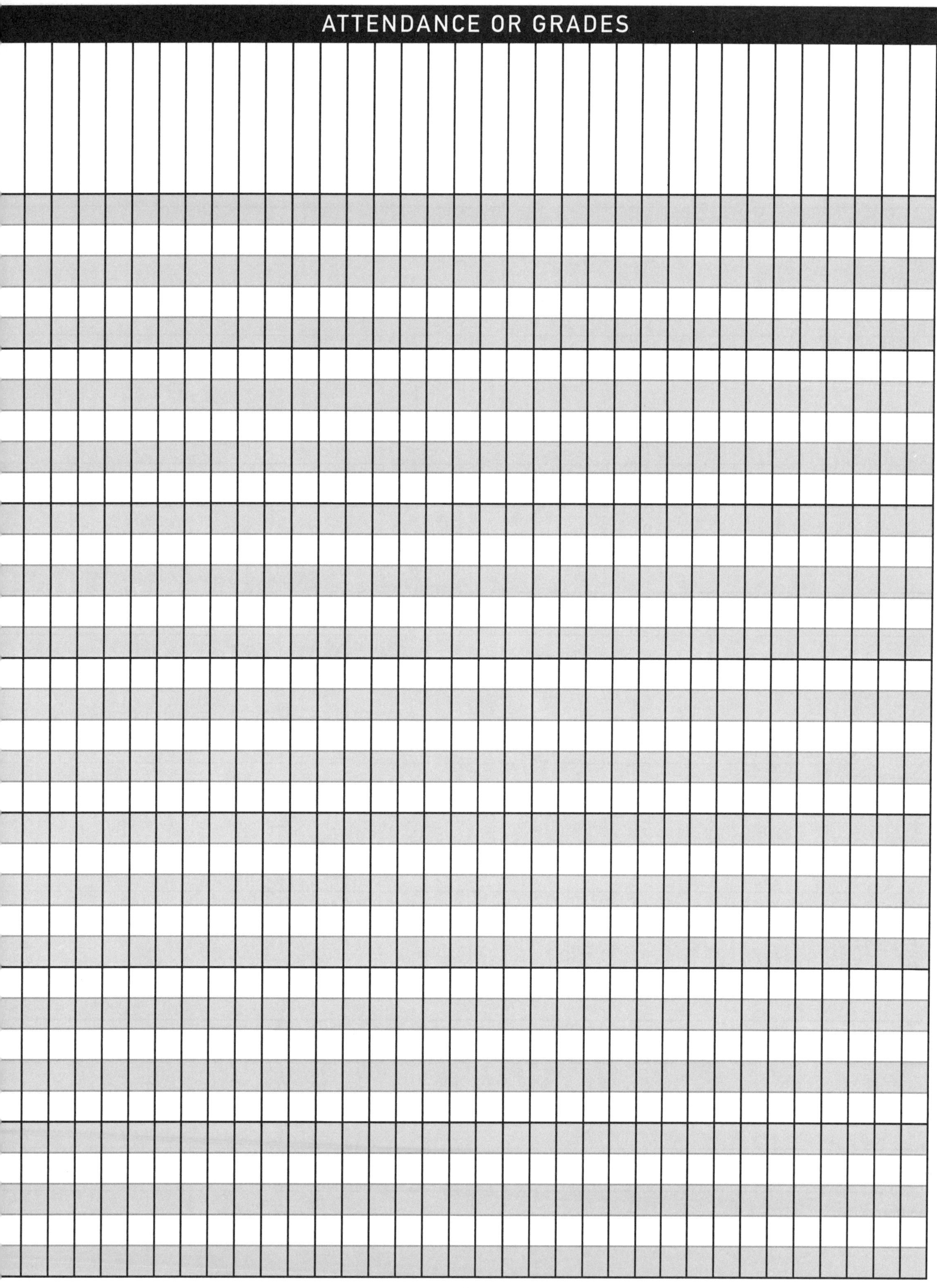

NOTES

NOTES

NOTES

NOTES

NOTES

NOTES

PETER PAUPER PRESS
Fine Books and Gifts Since 1928

Our Company

In 1928, at the age of twenty-two, Peter Beilenson began printing books on a small press in the basement of his parents' home in Larchmont, New York. Peter—and later, his wife, Edna—sought to create fine books that sold at "prices even a pauper could afford."

Today, still family owned and operated, Peter Pauper Press continues to honor our founders' legacy—and our customers' expectations—of beauty, quality, and value.

Cover design by Heather Zschock

Peter Pauper Press, Inc.
202 Mamaroneck Avenue
White Plains, NY 10601 USA

ISBN 978-1-4413-3126-7
Printed in China

7 6 5 4 3 2 1

Visit us at www.peterpauper.com